Tatted
JEWELRY™

Introduction

THREADS

The special thread used in these projects is Lizbeth, a 6-cord (cordonnet) type of thread. It has six plies—three sets of two twisted plies that are twisted yet again in the opposite direction. The result is a very smooth, durable thread with outstanding body.

Excellent tatting threads in a wide range of colors and sizes can be ordered from Handy Hands Tatting at www.hhtatting.com or found at shops specializing in tatting supplies. Six-cord threads are available in several brands including DMC Cordonnet Special, Flora, Olympus, Hakelgarn and others, but do be aware that even if the size number is the same, the thickness can vary in different brands. In general, the larger the size number, the finer the thread.

A number of artisans also hand-dye quality threads in every color combination imaginable. Look for their offerings at www.etsy.com—and while you're there, take a look at the inspiring tatting being done today.

TOOLS

Any kind of tatting shuttles can be used for these patterns. Very small crochet hooks are useful for joins as well as working with beads. One of my favorite craft tools isn't really intended for crafts at all—it's a floss threader, found in the dental-supply section of the drugstore. Floss threaders are handy for stringing beads that have holes too small to fit on even the smallest crochet hook.

BLOCKING TATTED JEWELRY

My blocking method is to lay the tatted piece on an ironing board and steam it. I don't touch it with the iron at all—just let the steam permeate the tatting, then set the iron aside and pat the tatting into shape. I steam both sides. Then, when satisfied with the appearance of the work, I turn it front side up, give it a final shot of steam and leave it to dry.

STIFFENING

People often ask me if I stiffen my tatted jewelry, and my answer is no, I usually don't. The 6-cord thread naturally produces a crisp piece of lace. But if an item does need extra stiffness, I'll paint fabric stiffener on the back of a finished piece only, using a small paintbrush and not touching the beads. I don't like stiffener on the front, because in my experience it dulls the shine of both the thread and the beads.

CARE

After a lot of wear, the tatted jewelry will eventually need to be washed. Simply wash by hand in sudsy water, rinse, reshape and lay out to dry.

JOINING TO A JEWELRY FINDING OPTIONS

A normal join will work for attaching the tatting to a split-ring finding (a metal ring coiled like a tiny key ring—this type of split ring is not the same thing as a tatted split ring). When joined that way, a regular jump ring needs to be added onto the split ring so that the finished piece faces the right way when worn. I like using split-ring findings with tatted jewelry because there are no openings where a thread might slip out.

Another option is to use pliers to attach a regular jump ring onto the tatting so that the jump ring encircles the tatted ring. Open a jump ring by twisting one end forward and the other back (not by pulling apart). Slip the tatted ring inside, and then twist the jump ring closed.

A third option is to use a special jewelry tool called split-ring pliers to open the coil of a metal split-ring finding so both working threads can be pushed inside the finding while the tatted ring is in the process of being made. The finished tatted ring will then have the metal coil encircling it.

WORKING WITH BEADS

Beads can be strung onto the thread before beginning, placed over picots or placed over the loop at the beginning of a self-closing mock ring.

If there are bead picots on a ring, the beads needed for the ring are slid up into the working circle of thread before beginning the ring. Keep the beads at the back of your hand until needed. Slide the bead into place when ready to make a bead picot (a picot with a bead dangling from it). Keep the remaining beads wound back a few turns on the shuttle to keep them out of your way until needed.

Beads can also be carried on the core thread between double stitches, as done in the connectors in the Celeste pattern. ■

Abbreviations

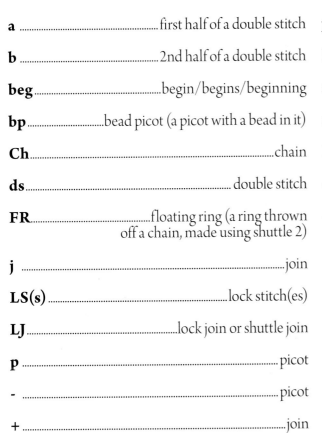

a	first half of a double stitch
b	2nd half of a double stitch
beg	begin/begins/beginning
bp	bead picot (a picot with a bead in it)
Ch	chain
ds	double stitch
FR	floating ring (a ring thrown off a chain, made using shuttle 2)
j	join
LS(s)	lock stitch(es)
LJ	lock join or shuttle join
p	picot
-	picot
+	join

prev	previous
R	ring
rep	repeat
rnd	round
RW	reverse work
SCMR	self-closing mock ring
SH	shuttle
SS	switch shuttles
st(s)	stitch(es)
vsp	very small picot
ZZ	zigzag or rickrack tatting, also known as "node stitch" or Victorian set stitches
[ ]	repeat the section in brackets number of times indicated

Tatting Guide

REVIEW OF FIRST HALF OF THE DOUBLE STITCH (a)

Under, over, through and **flip** *(transfer the loop to the thread wrapped around fingers by closing that your fingers a bit to loosen tension on the thread) (see Photo 1)*. The shuttle thread is the core that slides inside the double stitch *(see Photo 2)*; tighten tension on the core by pulling it straight *(see Photo 3)*. Slide the loop *(first half of a double stitch)* into place by opening your fingers to tighten *(see Photo 4)*.

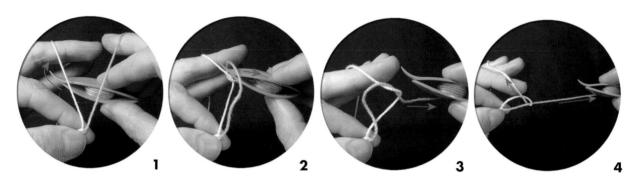

REVIEW OF 2ND HALF OF THE DOUBLE STITCH (b)

Over *(see Photo 5)*, under *(see Photo 6)*, through *(see Photo 7)* and flip *(see Photo 8)*.

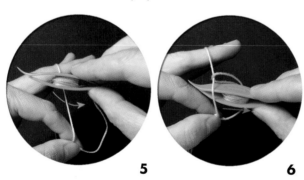
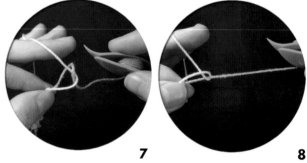

COMPLETED DOUBLE STITCH (DS)

Photo 9 shows the completed basic knot of tatting. It is referred to in knotting terminology as a lark's head on a running line.

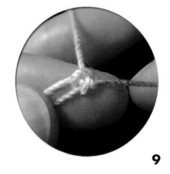

JOIN IN PROGRESS

The thread from your left hand may be pulled up though the picot **or** down; then the shuttle is slipped through. The direction of up or down changes the appearance a bit, but either way makes a **join that can slide.**

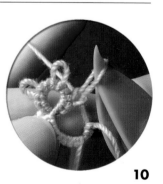

JOIN CONTINUED
Complete this type of join *(sometimes referred to as a "normal" join)* by making the 2nd half of a double stitch. Count the completed join as part of the next group of double stitches in the pattern.

11

LOCK JOIN IN PROGRESS (LJ)
This type of join is made by pulling the shuttle thread through the picot; it locks the tension. This type of join is usually **not** counted as a stitch.

12

RINGS & CHAINS
The two main parts of tatting patterns are **rings** and **chains**. To make a ring, pinch the shuttle thread between your thumb and forefinger, and then wrap it around your left fingers all the way back to thumb and forefinger to form a circle *(see Photo 13)*.

As you make double stitches you'll notice the circle around your fingers gets smaller as you use up the thread. Pull on the bottom of the circle, under your thumb, to make it bigger. After tatting the number of double stitches wanted, pull the shuttle to close the ring *(see Photo 14)*.

Reverse work means to turn your work so the thread will be in correct position to begin the next part of the pattern *(see Photo 15)*.

To tat a **chain**, wrap the ball thread *(or 2nd shuttle thread)* over your fingers, looping it around your little finger for tension *(see Photo 16)*.

Picots can be purely decorative or functional for joining. A picot is formed by leaving a space between two double stitches, and then sliding them together *(see Photo 17)*.

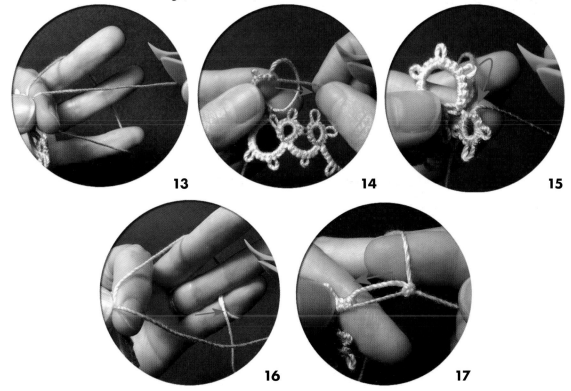

13 **14** **15** **16** **17**

HIDING ENDS

When the shuttle runs out of thread, you can **tat over the ends** to hide them. At the beginning of a ring, wrap the new shuttle thread around your fingers. *(It may not be necessary to tie a knot to the old thread, depending on the situation.)* Flip the first half of a double stitch, and then put the old end through alongside the core thread *(see Photo 18).*

Flip the 2nd half and put the old end through alongside the core *(see Photo 19).*

Continue for several double stitches, and then abandon the old end *(see Photo 20).* Wait to cut the protruding tail off until that area of the tatting is completed, so that the end doesn't work itself loose.

The new end that is left from starting the ring can be worked into the following chain in the same way.

Another way to hide ends is to sew them into the work. Thread the end into the smallest embroidery needle it will fit through and sew through the caps of the double stitches *(see Photo 21).*

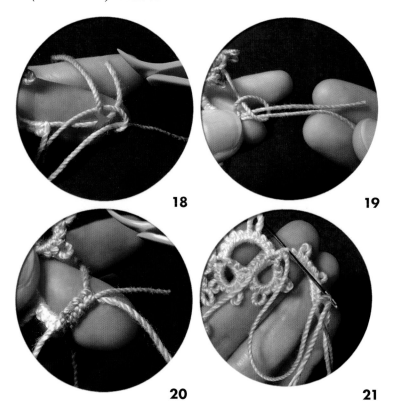

18

19

20

21

Carnival
Earrings

SKILL LEVEL

BEGINNER

FINISHED SIZE
1⅛ inches wide x 1½ inches long, excluding
earring finding

MATERIALS
- Size 20 Lizbeth thread (210 yds/
  25g per ball):
  6 yds #672 burgundy
- Plastic tatting shuttle
- Size 14/.75mm steel crochet hook
- Size 10 or 11 gold seed beads: 52
- 6mm round gold beads: 2
- 4mm round burgundy beads: 2
- Earring findings

SPECIAL TECHNIQUE
Lock stitch (LS): Work first half of ds unflipped
and 2nd half flipped.

INSTRUCTIONS
EARRING
MAKE 2.
*Notes: String beads on thread in the following order
before winding shuttle: 10 seed beads, 4mm bead
and 16 seed beads. Then wind shuttle, placing
beads a few turns back so they are out of the way
until needed.*

Slide up 3 beads, R 5, bp, 5, bp, 5, bp, 5, p, 10.

Slide up 3 beads, R 10, j to open p of prev R, 5,
bp with 3 seed beads, 5, p, 10.

Slide up next 9 beads, R 10, j to p of prev R, 5,
large bp with 9 beads, 5, p, 10.

Slide up 3 beads, R 10, j to p of prev R, 5, bp with
3 seed beads, 5, p, 10.

Slide up 3 beads, R 10, j to p of prev R, 5, bp, 5,
bp, 5, bp, 5.

Turn work.

Join 6mm round bead by inserting a crochet hook
through it, catching ball thread and pulling
it through bead. Keep pulling thread to get a
large enough loop to put shuttle through (*see
Photo A*).

PHOTO A

Complete join by pulling back on ball thread *(see Photo B)* until join is hidden inside bead *(see Photo C)*. Pull and wiggle both threads to get bead in place.

Keeping firm hold on bead, make a **LS** *(see Special Technique) (see Photo D)* centered at top of bead *(see Photo E)*.

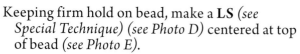

PHOTO B

PHOTO D

PHOTO C

PHOTO E

Continue with 4 LS.

Turn work.

TOP RING

Note: Ring contains 6 rem beads; ends are worked into this ring.

Slide up beads, R 2, bp, 2, bp, 2, bp, 2, j to finding, 2, bp, 2, bp, 2, bp, 2. ∎

Compass
Pendant

SKILL LEVEL

INTERMEDIATE

FINISHED SIZE
Pendant: 1¾ x 1¾ inches

MATERIALS
- Size 20 Lizbeth thread (210 yds/ 25g per ball):
  - 3 yds #661 country turquoise medium
  - 4 yds #604 black
- Plastic tatting shuttles: 2
- Size 14/.75mm steel crochet hook
- 6mm black round bead
- Paper clip
- 6mm split-ring finding and/or 1 jump ring
- Necklace chain with clasp

SPECIAL TECHNIQUE
Self-closing mock ring (SCMR): Beg tatting a chain, leaving large loop at beg. When number of double stitches needed have been tatted, put shuttle through loop and pull closed.

PATTERN NOTES
Pendant is tatted in 2 rounds, beginning at center with a self-closing mock ring around the 6mm bead. Floating rings are thrown off the self-closing mock ring with shuttle 2. Both rounds require 2 shuttles.

INSTRUCTIONS
PENDANT
Note: Wind about 2 yds of turquoise thread onto shuttle 2. Unwind about 1 yd of thread from ball; cut and wind this end on SH 1. The thread is continuous between the shuttles.

CENTER
Rnd 1: Begin with SCMR *(see Special Technique)*. Leaving large loop at beg, SCMR 6.

FR 4-3-4 *(see Photo A)*. Resume same SCMR, 6.

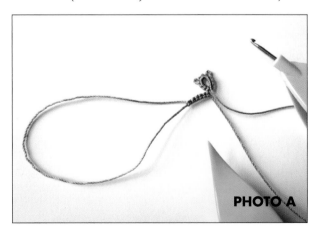

PHOTO A

Pull starting loop through bead with crochet hook, then put SH 1 through loop and tighten *(see Photo B)*.

Hint: A paper clip left in loop between bead and beg of tatting is helpful for saving a space for joining into later.

PHOTO B

[FR 4-3-4. Resume same SCMR, 6] twice.

Pull SH 1 thread to tighten SCMR around bead, remove paper clip and LJ to beg (see Photo C).

PHOTO C

FINAL FLOATING RING
Note: Work ends into this ring.

FR 4-3-4.

Note: Wind about 2 yds of black thread on each shuttle, leaving thread continuous between them. Shs frequently switch places in this rnd. They are numbered according to their working position at the time.

Rnd 2: Beg at top with Ch on a paper clip by sliding thread in paper clip and beg tatting *(paper clip holds a space for later joining).*

Ch 2-4. Pick up rnd 1 and hold it so that back side is facing you.

Using SH 2, LJ to first p *(when viewed from front side this is the 2nd p)* of any FR on center *(see Photo D).* RW, SS.

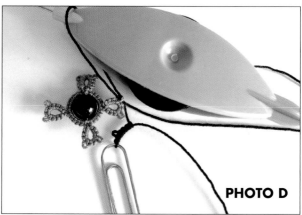

PHOTO D

*Ch 5.

FR 3-3.

Ch 5.

LJ with SH 1 to first p of next R of center. RW, SS.

Ch 4-2. RW.

Using SH 1, R 5-5. RW.

Ch 2+4 (j to p of prev Ch).

Using SH 2, LJ to next p of same R on center. RW, SS.

Rep from * around to beg of first Ch, joining p of last Ch to p of first Ch.

Remove paper clip and LJ with SH 1. RW.

FINAL RING
Note: Work ends into this ring.

R 5, j to finding, 5. ■

Lacy Treasure
Pendant

SKILL LEVEL

BEGINNER

FINISHED SIZE

Pendant: 1³⁄₈ inches wide x 1¹⁄₂ inches long

MATERIALS

Turquoise Version
- Size 10 Lizbeth thread (122 yds/
  25g per ball):
    4 yds #661 country turquoise medium
- Size 8 blue seed beads: 2
- 6mm–8mm green faceted bead
- Top-drilled teardrop bead
- Plastic tatting shuttle
- Size 14/.75mm steel crochet hook
- ¹⁄₂ yd ¹⁄₈-inch-wide black ribbon

- 4mm or 5mm jump rings: 3
- Wire cutters
- Jewelry pliers
- Necklace clasp
- Ribbon crimp ends

Beige Version
- Size 10 Lizbeth thread (122 yds/
  25g per ball):
    4 yds #693 linen medium
- Size 8 antique gold seed beads: 2
- 6mm–8mm round antique gold bead
- Antique gold charm
- Plastic tatting shuttle
- Size 14/.75mm steel crochet hook
- ¹⁄₂ yd ¹⁄₈-inch-wide black ribbon
- 4mm or 5mm jump rings: 3
- Wire cutters

- Jewelry pliers
- Necklace clasp
- Ribbon crimp ends

Variegated Version
- Size 10 Lizbeth thread (122 yds/ 25g per ball):
    4 yds #131 vineyard harvest
- Size 8 pink seed beads: 2
- 6mm–8mm round pink bead
- Top-drilled pink teardrop bead
- Plastic tatting shuttle
- Size 14/.75mm steel crochet hook
- ½ yd ⅛-inch-wide black ribbon
- 4mm or 5mm jump rings: 3
- Wire cutters
- Jewelry pliers
- Necklace clasp
- Ribbon crimp ends

INSTRUCTIONS
PENDANT
Notes: String 1 seed bead, 1 teardrop bead and 1 seed bead on thread. Wind shuttle, keeping beads on ball thread (no beads on SH). Large bead is sewn on after Pendant is completed.

[R 2-2-2-2-2-2 (5p). RW. Ch 2. RW] 3 times. *(Rings are not joined.)*

R 6, j to finding, 6.

RW. Ch 2.

LJ to base of first R. *(There is a tiny space that can be joined into with crochet hook—see Photo A)*

PHOTO A

Ch 6-2-2-2-2-2 *(5p).*

LJ to 3rd p of first R.

Ch 2-2-2-2.

LJ to 2nd p of next R.

Ch 2, bp *(see Photo B)*, 2, bp (teardrop bead), 2, bp, 2.

PHOTO B

LJ to 4th p of same R.

Ch 2-2-2-2.

LJ to 3rd p of next R.

Ch 2-2-2-2-2-6.

Leave long thread tails for last join and for sewing bead to Pendant *(see Photo C)*.

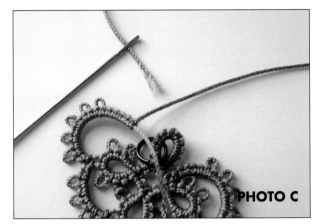

PHOTO C

FINISHING

Thread needle with core thread and sew it through base of ring with picots below. Tie threads.

Bring 1 thread back to front side of Pendant and string 6mm bead onto it. Sew thread with bead down through base of ring on opposite side of Pendant *(see Photo D)*.

PHOTO D

Tie both threads at back of Pendant in a square knot. Sew ends under caps of sts; trim ends.

Finish ends of ribbon with ribbon crimp ends. Add clasp with jump rings. ∎

One-Shuttle Glamour Earrings

SKILL LEVEL

INTERMEDIATE

FINISHED SIZE

¾ inch wide x 1½ inches long, excluding earring finding

MATERIALS

- Size 20 Lizbeth thread (210 yds/ 25g per ball):
  6 yds #693 linen medium
- Plastic tatting shuttle
- Size 14/.75mm steel crochet hook
- Size 11 seed beads: 66
- 6mm round beads: 2
- 4mm round beads: 2
- Paper clip
- Earring findings

SPECIAL TECHNIQUE

Self-closing mock ring (SCMR): Beg tatting a chain, leaving large loop at beg. When the number of double stitches needed have been tatted, put shuttle through loop and pull closed.

PATTERN NOTE

For long beaded picot, place indicated number of beads on crochet hook and pull thread from working thread around left hand through them. Secure temporarily with paper clip.

INSTRUCTIONS
EARRING
MAKE 2.

Notes: String beads on thread in the following order: 5 seed beads, 4mm round bead and 5 seed beads. Wind shuttle, leaving all strung beads on ball thread.

Beg with a SCMR *(see Special Technique)*, leaving large loop at beg (it may be helpful to leave a paper clip in the loop).

SCMR 6, vsp, 2, long beaded picot with 4 seed beads *(see Pattern Note)*.

Resume same SCMR, 2, long beaded p with 5 seed beads, 2.

Slip 6mm round bead over beg loop *(leave paper clip in as a space saver)*, put shuttle through loop *(see Photo A)* and pull loop up tightly to bead.

PHOTO A

Note: Bead is tatted halfway around at this point. Continue around other half of center bead.

Resume SCMR, 2, long beaded p with 5 seed beads, 2, long beaded p with 5 seed beads, 2, long beaded p with 4 seed beads, 2, vsp, 6.

Pull SCMR up tightly, then remove paper clip and LJ to base of round bead.

Do not RW.

OUTER ROUND
Ch 7, LJ to vsp.

Ch 7, LJ to next bp.

Ch 7. RW.

R 3, j to center bp, 3. RW.

Ch 7. RW.

R 7, j to next bp, 7. RW *(see Photo B)*.

PHOTO B

Large beaded p with all beads from ball thread in it, Ch 7. RW.

R 3, j to next bp, 3. RW.

Ch 7. LJ to next bp.

Ch 7, LJ to vsp.

Ch 7.

LJ to beg. Do not RW.

TOP RING
Note: Work ends into this ring.

R 5, j to finding, 5. ∎

Celeste
Necklace & Earrings

SKILL LEVEL

EXPERIENCED

FINISHED SIZES
Necklace: 16 inches long
Earrings: 1½ inches long,
   excluding earring finding

MATERIALS
- Size 10 Lizbeth thread (122 yds/
   25g per ball):
      20 yds #131 vineyard harvest
- Plastic tatting shuttles: 2
- Size 14/.75mm steel crochet hook
- Size 8 seed beads: 55
- 6mm round bead
- 3 paper clips
- ¾ yd ⅛-inch-wide beige ribbon
- 5-inch length necklace chain with
   end cap
- 4mm or 5mm jump rings: 10
- Wire cutters
- Jewelry pliers
- Necklace clasp
- Ribbon crimp ends
- Earring findings

SPECIAL TECHNIQUE
Self-closing mock ring (SCMR): Beg tatting a
   chain, leaving large loop at beg. When number
   of double stitches needed have been tatted, put
   shuttle through loop and pull closed.

PATTERN NOTES
Center Motif is tatted in 2 pieces that are joined
   as they are tatted. Begin with a self-closing
mock ring around a 6mm bead. Lower ring is
floated off first half of self-closing mock ring
and features long picots covered with beads
that are temporarily secured with paper clips
before being joined to outer chains.

Tatted Connectors are made using a shuttle
   and ball. Separate pieces of Necklace are put
   together with jump rings.

INSTRUCTIONS
NECKLACE
CENTER MOTIF

Notes: String 8 seed beads on thread before winding shuttles. Wind 2 shuttles full, leaving thread continuous between them and sliding all beads a few turns back on SH 2.

SCMR (*see Special Technique*) 4, leaving a large loop at beg.

FR 3, slide bead in place, 3.

Notes: To form long beaded picot, place some beads on crochet hook and pull thread through them (from the working thread around left hand). Rep until 10 beads are on thread. Secure temporarily with paper clip. Tighten tension on beads enough so that they are close together, but leave a little slack so that they can bend (see Photo A). Then resume tatting.

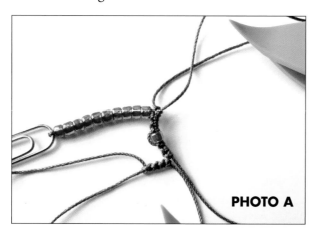

PHOTO A

Continue same FR with [3, slide bead in place] 3 times.

Finish FR with 3, another long beaded p, 3, slide bead in place, 3. Close FR.

Resume SCMR by tatting 4 ds. Slip 6mm bead over beg loop, put shuttle 1 through loop (*see Photo B*) and pull loop snug to bead.

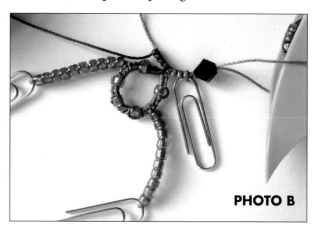

PHOTO B

Hint: A paper clip can be left between start of tatting and bead to keep a space open for easier joining later. You have tatted halfway around the bead at this point.

Resume SCMR (continuing around other half of center bead).

Leave a vsp at right at end of bead, 8.

Pull SCMR up tightly, then remove paper clip and LJ to base of bead (*see Photo C*). RW, SS.

PHOTO C

UPPER CHAIN
Note: Upper chain has 5 floating rings.

Ch 3-3.

FR 2-2-2-2.

[Ch 3 *(see Photo D)*. FR 2+2-2-2 (j to last p of prev FR)] 4 times.

Ch 2, bp, 2, bp *(see Photo F)*, 2, bp, 2. RW.

PHOTO F

R 4+2+4-4 (first j to open p on upper Ch, 2nd j to last p on FR). RW.

Ch 4, j to long beaded p *(see Photo G)*, 4. RW.

PHOTO D

Ch 3-3.

LJ to vsp at end of center bead *(see Photo E)*. RW, SS.

PHOTO G

PHOTO E

Hints: If you wish to maintain a "front side, back side" appearance, work next Ch by tatting each ds with 2nd half followed by first half.

Or another option is to tat this Ch normally and change to 2nd half, first half on corresponding Ch of opposite side.

TREFOIL
R 4+5-2 (j to last p of prev R).

R 2+7-2 (j to last p of prev R).

LAST RING
Note: Work ends into this ring.

Last R 2+9 (j to last p of prev R).

OPPOSITE SIDE OF MOTIF
Notes: Work this side with only 1 shuttle and ball thread. There will probably be enough thread left on 1 shuttle, so just unwind about a yard from that shuttle to use as the "ball" thread, leaving it attached to shuttle. String 3 seed beads on ball thread.

Turn piece so that it is reversed and back side up—ready to continue the tatting on other side.

LJ to vsp at other side of 6mm bead.

Ch 2, bp, 2, bp, 2, bp, 2. RW.

R 4+2+4-4 (first j to open p on upper Ch, 2nd j to last p on FR). RW.

Ch 4, j to long beaded p, 4. RW.

TREFOIL
R 4+5-2 (j to last p of prev R).

R 2+7-2 (j to last p of prev R).

LAST R
Note: Work ends into this ring.

Last R 2+9 (j to last p of prev R).

CONNECTOR
MAKE 2.
Note: These require only 1 shuttle and ball thread. String 6 seed beads on thread and slide all beads a few turns back on shuttle.

R 2-7-2.

[R 2+7-2 (j to last p of prev R)] twice. Do not RW.

Ch first half of a ds unflipped. Then continue tatting normally.

Ch 2, j to last p of prev R, 2, [slide a bead in place, 2] twice, slide a bead in place, 2-2. Do not RW.

R 2+7-2 (j to last p of prev Ch).

[R 2+7-2 (j to last p of prev R)] twice. Do not RW.

Ch first half of a ds unflipped. Then continue tatting normally.

Ch 2, j to last p of prev R, [slide a bead in place, 2] twice, slide a bead in place, 2+2 (j to first p of first R).

Tie threads around base of Trefoil and sew in ends.

FINISHING
With wire cutters, cut 2 pieces of metal chain about 1 inch each. Attach 1 chain piece to center ring of Trefoil on each side of Center Motif with 1 jump ring. Then use jump rings to attach center ring of 1 tatted Connector to each chain. Also place 1 jump ring on center ring at other end of Connector.

Cut 2 pieces of ribbon about 11 inches long. Fold each piece in half and knot to jump ring at end of tatted Connector. Lay necklace out to measure the length and trim ribbons shorter if necessary.

Finish ends of ribbon with ribbon crimp ends. Add clasp with jump rings. Add 3-inch length of necklace chain to jump ring.

EARRING
MAKE 2.
Work same as Connector for Necklace.

FINISHING
Add 1 jump ring and finding to top of each Connector. ∎

Giddy
Earrings

SKILL LEVEL

INTERMEDIATE

FINISHED SIZE
1 inch wide x 1½ inches long, excluding
earring finding

MATERIALS
- Size 20 Lizbeth thread (210 yds/
  25g per ball):
    6 yds #620 azalea medium
- Plastic tatting shuttles: 2
- Size 14/.75mm steel crochet hook
- Size 11 pink seed beads: 30
- 6mm pink round beads: 2
- 4mm pink round beads: 2
- Earring findings

SPECIAL TECHNIQUE
Self-closing mock ring (SCMR): Beg tatting
a chain, leaving large loop at beg. When
the number of double stitches needed have
been tatted, put shuttle through loop and
pull closed.

INSTRUCTIONS
EARRING
MAKE 2.
*Notes: String beads on thread in the following order
before winding shuttles: 4 seed beads, 4mm bead
and 11 seed beads. Wind about 1 yd on SH 1,
then measure off about 2 yds of thread from ball
and wind on SH 2. All of beads will be on SH 2
thread. SH 2 is not used until middle of project,
so do not wind beads on it yet. There are no beads
on SH 1.*

CENTER
Beg with **SCMR** *(see Special Technique)*, leaving
large loop at beg.

SCMR 2-2-2-2-2-2 *(5p)*. Slip 6mm bead over beg
loop *(see Photo A)* put SH 1 through loop *(see
Photo B)* *(leave a paper clip in as a space saver)*,
and pull loop up snug to bead *(see Photo C)*.

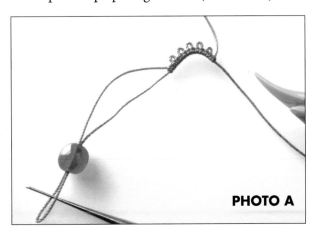
PHOTO A

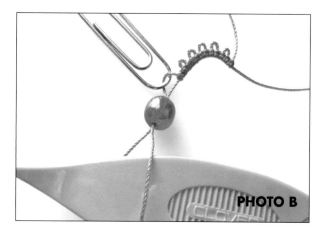

PHOTO B

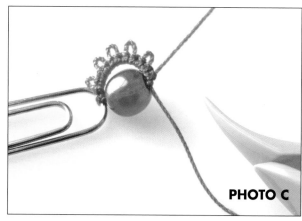

PHOTO C

Resume SCMR (continuing around lower side of bead) 2, bp, 2-2, bp, 2-2, bp, 2-2, bp, 2-2, bp, 2-2, bp, 2-2, bp, 2.

Pull SCMR up snug, then remove paper clip and LJ to base of bead *(see Photo D)*. Do not RW.

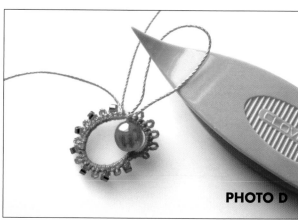

PHOTO D

OUTER ROUND
TOP
Ch 2-2-2-2-2.

FR 6, j to finding, 6.

Ch 2-2-2-2-2. LJ to end of 6mm bead.

CONTINUING OUTER ROUND
[Ch 2-2-2-2. LJ to the next open p] 3 times.

BOTTOM CENTER
2-2; large bp of 4 seed beads, 4mm bead and 4 seed beads; then 2-2. LJ to next open p.

[Ch 2-2-2-2. LJ to next open p] twice. Ch 2-2-2-2, LJ to start.

Tie, hide ends and cut. ∎

Keyed Up
Earrings & Necklace

SKILL LEVEL

BEGINNER

FINISHED SIZES
Pendant: 1¼ inches wide x 1½ inches long
Earring: 1½ inches long, excluding
   earring finding

MATERIALS
Beige Version Earrings
- Size 20 Lizbeth thread (210 yds/ 25g per ball):
   6 yds #693 linen medium
- Plastic tatting shuttles: 2
- Size 14/.75mm steel crochet hook
- Size 11 antique gold seed beads: 6
- 4mm or 5mm jump ring
- Small charms: 2
- Earring findings

Red Version Earrings
- Size 20 Lizbeth thread (210 yds/ 25g per ball):
   6 yds #671 Christmas red
- Plastic tatting shuttles: 2
- Size 14/.75mm steel crochet hook
- Size 11 gold seed beads: 6
- Top-drilled red dagger beads: 2
- 4mm or 5mm jump ring
- Earring findings

Black Version Necklace & Earrings
- Size 20 Lizbeth thread (210 yds/ 25g per ball):
   6 yds #604 black
- Size 10 Lizbeth thread (122 yds/ 25g per ball):
   6 yds #604 black
- Plastic tatting shuttles: 2
- Size 14/.75mm steel crochet hook
- Size 11 red seed beads: 6
- Size 8 red seed beads: 3
- Top-drilled red dagger beads: 3
- 4mm or 5mm jump ring
- 20-inch length necklace chain with end cap
- Necklace clasp
- Earring findings

INSTRUCTIONS
EARRING
MAKE 2.

Notes: String 3 size 11 seed beads on size 20 thread. Wind 2 shuttles, having 3 size 11 seed beads on SH 1.

CENTER RING

Note: For advanced tatters, if you tat front side/back side, this pattern is easier to work if first ring is tatted "back side" using 2nd half of ds followed by first half.

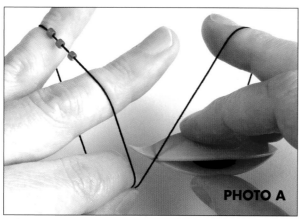

When tatting a ring with bead picots, slide number of beads needed in working circle of thread around left fingers before beginning ring. Keep beads at back of hand until needed *(see Photo A)*.

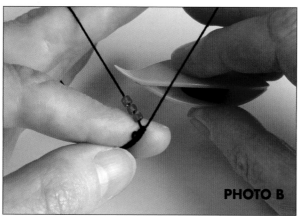

Slide beads in place when ready to make a bead picot *(see Photo B)*.

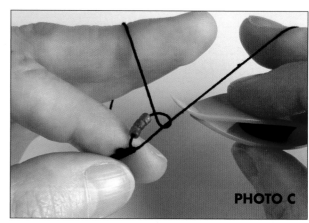

Tighten picot around beads *(see Photo C)*.

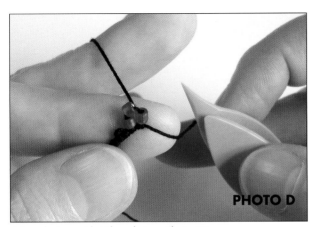

A bead picot with 3 beads (see Photo D).

Slide up 3 seed beads, R 7-2, bp with 3 seed beads, 2-7. RW.

Ch 2-2-2-2-2-2 (5p). SS; do not RW.

R 11-3 (see Photo E). RW.

Ch 3+3 (j to p of Center Ring). RW.

R 3+8-3 (j to p of prev R). RW.

Ch 4. RW.

BOTTOM RING
R 2+16-2 (j to p of prev R). RW.

Ch 4. RW.

R 3+8-3 (j to p of prev R). RW.

Ch 3+3 (j to p of Center Ring). RW.

R 3+11 (j to p of prev R). SS; do not RW.

Ch 2-2-2-2-2-2 (5p). LJ to beg.

TOP RING
Note: Work ends into this ring.

R 7, j to finding, 7.

FINISHING
Attach a dagger bead or charm with a jump ring to Bottom Ring of each Earring.

NECKLACE
PENDANT
With size 10 black thread and size 8 red seed beads, work same as Earring, joining Top Ring to jump ring instead of finding.

FINISHING
Attach red dagger bead with jump ring to Bottom Ring of Pendant. Attach necklace to jump ring at top of Pendant. ■

Newcastle
Necklace

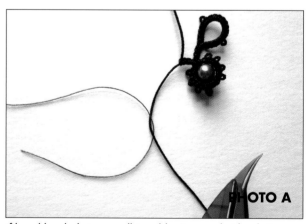

EXPERIENCED

FINISHED SIZE

1¾ inches wide x 8 inches long

MATERIALS

- Size 10 Lizbeth thread (122 yds/ 25g per ball):
  24 yds #604 black
  15 yds #678 olive dark
- Plastic tatting shuttle
- Size 14/.75mm steel crochet hook
- 6mm gold round beads: 3
- Size 8 black seed beads: 51
- Size 8 beige seed beads: 12
- 5mm–6mm jump rings: 3
- 5mm–6mm split rings: 2
- Paper clips
- 10-inch length necklace chain with end cap
- Necklace clasp
- Purchased charm

SPECIAL TECHNIQUE

Alligator join: Pass shuttle thread over work and ball thread under work before beg next st. The tatting inside this join is squeezed in between 2 double stitches.

PATTERN NOTES

Necklace is tatted in 2 rounds, using 1 shuttle and ball of thread for each round.

Work proceeds clockwise, with top of right wing worked first, and then lower side. Continue with lower side of left wing and then top of left wing.

INSTRUCTIONS
PENDANT

Notes: Wind shuttle full with black. Start with Center Ring (to which pendant will be attached).

CENTER RING

R 5-5, j to finding, 5-5. RW.

Ch 5. RW.

PHOTO A

If bead has hole too small to add using crochet hook, it can be added using a piece of sewing thread and a floss threader or beading needle. Fold sewing thread over tatting thread, in this instance, shuttle thread *(see Photo A)*.

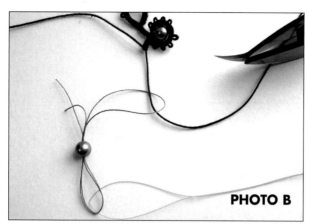

Put sewing thread, doubled, through eye of floss threader or beading needle. Slide bead onto needle and down sewing thread *(see Photo B).*

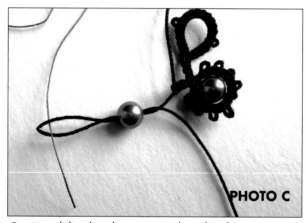

Continue sliding bead onto tatting thread and remove sewing thread *(see Photo C).*

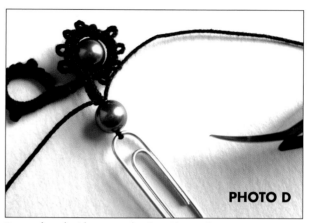

Secure bead with paper clip *(see Photo D).*

BEADED RINGS

Note: Prepare next ring for bead in center by pulling loop of shuttle thread through bead, then secure loop with paper clip and tighten. Tat ring as usual, keeping bead below work.

R 2-2-2-2-2, remove paper clip and join *(normal join)* to end of loop sticking out of bead. Then continue R with 2-2-2-2-2. Close R around bead. RW.

Ch 3, RW. Work 2nd beaded R in same way *(see Photo E),* except j first p of R to last p of prev R. RW.

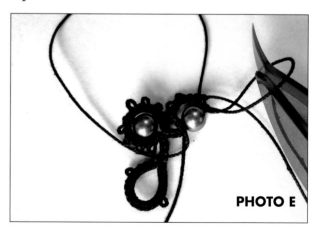

Ch 3, RW. Work 3rd beaded R in same way, j first p of R to last p of prev R. RW.

Ch 5. LJ to base of Center Ring. RW.

RIGHT WING
TOP
Ch 10. RW.

R 2-2-2-2-2-2 (5p). RW.

Ch 4+2-2 (j to 4th last p of last beaded R). RW.

R 2-2+2-2-2-2 (j to 2nd last p of prev R). RW.

Ch 2-2-2-2. RW.

LARGE RINGS SECTION
Note: Place a size 8 bead over each on large rings. Bead can be secured temporarily with a paper clip until ready to join to beaded picot (see Photo F).

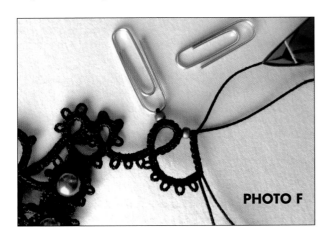

PHOTO F

R 6-4-6. RW.

[Ch 2-2-2-2-2-2 (5p). RW. R 6+4-6 (j to last p of prev R). RW] twice.

Ch 2-2-2-2. RW.

SMALL RINGS SECTION
R 2-2-2-2-2-2 (5p). RW.

Ch 2-2-2-2. RW.

R 2-2+2-2-2-2 (j to 2nd last p of prev R). RW.

WING TIP
Ch 2-2-2-2-2-2 (5p). Do not RW.

R 8, j to jump ring, 8. Do not RW.

LOWER SIDE
Ch 2-2-2-2-2-2 (5p). RW.

SMALL RINGS SECTION
R 2-2-2+2-2-2 (j to 3rd p of opposite R). RW.

Ch 2-2-2-2. RW.

R 2-2+2+2-2-2 (first j to 2nd last p of prev R, next j to 3rd p of opposite R). RW.

Ch 2-2-2-2. RW.

LARGE RINGS SECTION
[R 6+4-6 (j to last p of prev large R). RW. Ch 2-2-2-2-2-2 (5p). RW] twice.

R 6+4+6 (first j to last p of prev R, 2nd j to p of opposite R). RW.

Ch 2-2-2-2. RW.

SMALL RINGS
Note: These rings are near center.

R 2-2-2+2-2-2 (j to 3rd p of opposite R). RW.

Ch 2-2-2-2. RW.

R 2-2+2+2-2-2 (first j to 2nd last p of prev R, next j to 3rd p of opposite R). RW.

BOTTOM
Ch 2-2-2-2-2-2-2-2 (7p). LJ to nearest p of Center Ring.

RW, keeping ball thread below work. *(Pull enough of ball thread up to top to be able to work next chain.)*

Ch 7.

Alligator join *(see Special Technique)* around base of Center Ring with ball thread below work, shuttle thread above.

Ch 7. LJ to next p of Center Ring. RW.

Ch 2-2-2-2-2-2-2-2 (7p). RW.

LOWER SIDE
R 2-2-2-2-2-2 (5p). RW.

Ch 2-2-2-2. RW.

R 2-2+2-2-2-2 (j to 2nd last p of prev R). RW.

Ch 2-2-2-2. RW (*see Photo G—also shows start of large rings section*).

PHOTO G

LARGE RINGS SECTION
Note: *Place a size 8 bead over each picot on large rings. Bead can be secured temporarily with a paper clip until ready to join to beaded picot.*

R 6-4-6. RW.

[Ch 2-2-2-2-2-2 (5p). RW. R 6+4-6 (j to last p of prev R). RW] twice.

Ch 2-2-2-2. RW.

SMALL RINGS SECTION
R 2-2-2-2-2-2 (5p). RW.

Ch 2-2-2-2. RW.

R 2-2+2-2-2-2 (j to 2nd last p of prev R). RW.

WING TIP
Ch 2-2-2-2-2-2 (5p). Do not RW.

R 8, j to jump ring, 8. Do not RW.

TOP
Ch 2-2-2-2-2-2 (5p). RW.

SMALL RINGS SECTION
R 2-2-2+2-2-2 (j to 3rd p of opposite R). RW.

Ch 2-2-2-2. RW.

R 2-2+2+2-2-2 (first j to 2nd last p of prev R, next j to 3rd p of opposite R). RW.

Ch 2-2-2-2. RW.

LARGE RINGS SECTION
[R 6+4-6 (j to last p of prev large R). RW. Ch 2-2-2-2-2 (5p). RW] twice.

R 6+4+6 (first j to last p of prev R, 2nd j to p of opposite R). RW.

Ch 2-2-2-2. RW.

SMALL RINGS
Note: *These rings are near center.*

R 2-2-2+2-2-2 (j to 3rd p of opposite R). RW.

Ch 2-2+4 (j to 4th last p of last beaded R) (*see Photo H*). RW.

PHOTO H

R 2-2+2+2-2-2 (first j to 2nd last p of prev R, next j to 3rd p of opposite R). RW.

Ch 10. LJ to beg, tie ends, hide and cut.

BORDER
Note: *String 51 beads on olive thread before winding shuttle. Since this rnd is all chains, wind only about 2 yds on shuttle, leaving rest of thread with beads attached to ball.*

LEFT WING UPPER SIDE
Hold piece with RS facing, LJ to first p at upper tip of Left Wing.

[Ch 3, bp, 3. LJ to 2nd p] twice *(see Photo I)*.

PHOTO I

Ch 1, LJ to first p of next Ch.

[Ch 3, bp, 3, LJ to 2nd p. Ch 1, LJ to first p of next Ch] twice.

[Ch 3, bp, 3. LJ to 2nd p] twice.

Ch 1, LJ to first p of next Ch.

[Ch 3, bp, 3. LJ to 2nd p] twice.

Ch 1, LJ to first p of next Ch.

Ch 3, bp, 3, LJ to 2nd p. Ch 1, LJ to first p of next Ch.

CENTER

Ch 3, bp, 3, LJ to 2nd open p of beaded R.

Ch 1, LJ to 2nd open p of middle beaded R.

[Ch 3, bp, 3, LJ to next p of middle beaded R] 3 times.

Ch 1, LJ to 2nd open p of next beaded R.

Ch 3, bp, 3, LJ to open p of next Ch.

RIGHT WING UPPER SIDE

Ch 1, LJ to first p of next Ch.

Ch 3, bp, 3, LJ to 2nd p. Ch 1, LJ to first p of next Ch.

[Ch 3, bp, 3. LJ to 2nd p] twice.

Ch 1, LJ to first p of next Ch.

[Ch 3, bp, 3. LJ to 2nd p] twice.

Ch 1, LJ to first p of next Ch.

[Ch 3, bp, 3, LJ to 2nd p. Ch 1, LJ to first p of next Ch] twice.

[Ch 3, bp, 3. LJ to 2nd p] twice.

RING WING TIP
Ch 3, bp, 3, LJ to first p of next Ch.

RIGHT WING LOWER SIDE
[Ch 3, bp, 3. LJ to 2nd p] twice.

Ch 1, LJ to first p of next Ch.

[Ch 3, bp, 3, LJ to 2nd p. Ch 1, LJ to first p of next Ch] twice.

[Ch 3, bp, 3. LJ to 2nd p] twice.

Ch 1, LJ to first p of next Ch.

[Ch 3, bp, 3. LJ to 2nd p] twice.

Ch 1, LJ to first p of next Ch.

[Ch 3, bp, 3, LJ to 2nd p. Ch 1, LJ to first p of next Ch] twice.

[Ch 3, bp, 3. LJ to 2nd p] 3 times.

BOTTOM CENTER
Ch 8. LJ to first p of next Ch.

LEFT WING LOWER SIDE
[Ch 3, bp, 3. LJ to 2nd p] 3 times.

Ch 1, LJ to first p of next Ch.

[Ch 3, bp, 3, LJ to 2nd p. Ch 1, LJ to first p of next Ch] twice.

[Ch 3, bp, 3. LJ to 2nd p] twice.

Ch 1, LJ to first p of next Ch.

[Ch 3, bp, 3. LJ to 2nd p] twice.

Ch 1, LJ to first p of next Ch.

[Ch 3, bp, 3, LJ to 2nd p. Ch 1, LJ to first p of next Ch] twice.

[Ch 3, bp, 3. LJ to 2nd p] twice.

Ch 3, bp, 3, LJ to beg. Tie ends, hide and cut.

FINISHING
Use jump ring to attach charm to Center Ring at bottom center of Pendant.

Cut 2 pieces of necklace chain about 5 inches long. Use jump ring to attach 1 piece of chain to split ring of tatted ring at tip of each Wing. Attach necklace clasp to end of chain. ■

Trendy Teardrop Earrings & Necklace

SKILL LEVEL

◼◼◼◻
EXPERIENCED

FINISHED SIZES

Earrings: 1 inch wide x 1¾ inches long, excluding earring finding
Pendant: 1¾ inches wide x 2 inches long

MATERIALS

Earrings
- Size 20 Lizbeth thread (210 yds/25g per ball):
  - 8 yds #682 country grape dark
- Plastic tatting shuttles: 2
- Size 14/.75mm steel crochet hook
- 4mm gold round beads: 2
- Paper clips: 2
- Earring findings

Necklace
- Size 10 Lizbeth thread (122 yds/25g per ball):
  - 4 yds #682 country grape dark
- Plastic tatting shuttles: 2
- Size 14/.75mm steel crochet hook
- 6mm round bead
- 6mm split-ring finding and/or 1 jump ring
- 20-inch necklace chain with end cap
- Necklace clasp

SPECIAL TECHNIQUES

Self-closing mock ring (SCMR): Beg tatting a chain, leaving large loop at beg. When the number of double stitches needed have been tatted, put shuttle through loop and pull closed.

Zigzag (ZZ): Work half of a double stitch the number of times given, followed by the other half repeated the number of times given, completing 1 set.

Catherine wheel join (CWJ): To work this joining see photos F–J on pages 32 and 33.

PATTERN NOTES

In this pattern, joins are not included in stitch count.

Chains are worked in zigzag. The rings are worked in standard tatting.

INSTRUCTIONS
EARRING
MAKE 2.

Notes: Wind about 3 yds of thread on SH 2. Then unwind about a yd of thread from ball; cut and wind this end on SH 1. Thread is continuous between shuttles. All picots are very small picots. Floating rings are made using SH 2.

Beg with open end chain, putting thread through a paper clip so that a space is held for joining into later. Pull core of chain occasionally while working to keep tension tight.

Rnd 1: ZZ (*see Special Techniques*) Ch 2**a** (*see Tatting Guide*), 3**b** (*see Tatting Guide*), p (*leave a space to form p; this is "drop p" because it shows on bottom side of Ch*), 3a, 2b.

Continue same ZZ Ch with [2a, 2b] twice.

ZZ Ch 1b, drop p with bead, 3a, 2b, 2a, 2b.

Hint: Slip bead on picot while in progress and secure temporarily with paper clip (see Photo A).

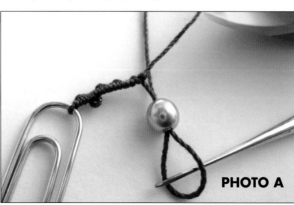

PHOTO A

FR 3-3 (*see Photo B*).

ZZ Ch [2a, 2b] twice.

FR 6-6.

ZZ Ch [2a, 2b] twice.

FR 10-10.

ZZ Ch [2a, 2b] twice.

FR 14-14 (*this is bottom center ring.*)

ZZ Ch [2a, 2b] twice.

FR 10-10.

ZZ Ch [2a, 2b] twice.

FR 6-6.

ZZ Ch [2a, 2b] twice.

FR 3-3.

ZZ Ch 2a, 2b, 2a, 3b. Remove paper clip from beaded drop p, and join *(normal join) (see Photos C and D).* Then ZZ Ch 3a, 2b.

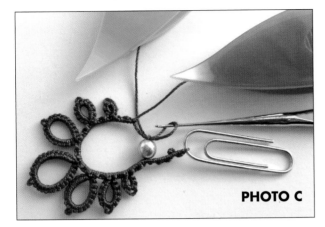

PHOTO C

PHOTO D

Continue same ZZ Ch [2a, 2b] twice.

Then ZZ Ch 1b, j to first drop p *(see Photo E),* 3a, 2b.

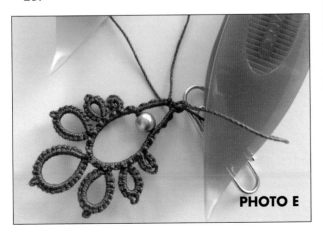

PHOTO E

Check tension of work and pull core thread to tighten as needed. Then remove paper clip and LJ to end of chain.

LS twice. *(First half of a ds not flipped, 2nd half flipped normally—or vice versa.)*

Do not RW.

Rnd 2: Leave a vsp, then ZZ Ch [2a, 2b] 8 times.

Note: The following 5 photos show a CWJ in progress.

PHOTO F

Pull shuttle 2 thread through picot, (under core thread) and put shuttle 2 through loop *(see Photo F).*

PHOTO G

The shuttle 1 thread (core) is enclosed *(see Photo G).*

"Pop" loop through to back by pulling on thread coming from chain *(see Photo H).*

Pull up on "popped through" loop to form and tighten the first half of a double stitch. Then put shuttle 2 through loop and pull shuttle 2 thread to form and tighten 2nd half of a double stitch *(see Photo I).*

Core (shuttle 1 thread) slides inside completed Catherine wheel join *(see Photo J).*

CWJ to p of first R.

ZZ Ch [2a, 2b] 3 times.

CWJ to p of next R.

ZZ Ch [2a, 2b] 4 times.

CWJ to p of next R.

ZZ Ch [2a, 2b] 5 times.

CWJ to p of next R. *(this is bottom center).*

ZZ Ch [2a, 2b] 5 times.

CWJ to p of next R.

ZZ Ch [2a, 2b] 4 times.

CWJ to p of next R.

ZZ Ch [2a, 2b] 3 times.

CWJ to p of next R *(this is last ring on rnd 1).*

ZZ Ch [2a, 2b] 8 times.

Adjust tension of chain by pulling on core thread, then LJ to p at beg of rnd 2.

FINAL RING
Note: Final ring at top is made with SH 1. Work ends into this ring.

R 6, j to finding, 6.

NECKLACE
PENDANT
With size 10 thread, work same as Earring.

FINISHING
Add split ring or jump ring to top of Pendant. Add Pendant to necklace chain. ∎

Belle
Pendant

SKILL LEVEL

INTERMEDIATE

FINISHED SIZE
1½ wide x 2 inches long

MATERIALS
- Size 20 Lizbeth thread (210 yds/ 25g per ball):
    7 yds #624 raspberry pink medium
- Plastic tatting shuttle: 2
- Size 14/.75mm steel crochet hook
- Size 10 or 11 black seed beads: 33
- 6mm black round bead
- Top-drilled black dagger bead
- ½ yd ⅛-inch-wide black ribbon
- Paper clips
- 4mm or 5mm jump rings: 3
- Jewelry pliers
- 2-inch length necklace chain with end cap
- Necklace clasp
- Ribbon crimp ends

SPECIAL TECHNIQUE
Self-closing mock ring (SCMR): Beg tatting a chain, leaving large loop at beg. When number of double stitches needed have been tatted, put shuttle through loop and pull closed.

PATTERN NOTE
For long beaded picot, place indicated number of beads on crochet hook and pull thread from working thread around left hand through them. Secure temporarily with paper clip.

INSTRUCTIONS
PENDANT
Notes: String beads onto thread in the following order before winding shuttle: 21 seed beads, dagger bead and 12 seed beads. Wind SH 2 first, putting on about 4 yds of thread. Then cut about 3 yds from ball and wind SH 1. All strung beads are on shuttle 2.

CENTER
SCMR (*see Special Technique*), 12, leaving large loop at beg (*it may be helpful to leave a paper clip in that loop*). Slip 6mm bead over beg loop (*leave the paper clip in as a space saver*), put shuttle through loop (*see Photo A*) and pull loop up snug to bead. Bead is tatted halfway around at this point.

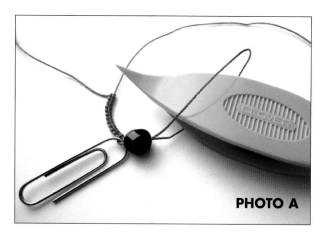

PHOTO A

Resume SCMR with vsp, 12. Pull SCMR up snug, then remove paper clip and LJ to base of bead (see Photo B). Do not RW.

PHOTO B

Rnd 1: Ch 2-2-2-2-2-2-2-2-2 (7p). LJ to vsp bp of 3 seed beads.

Ch 2-2-2-2-2-2-2-2-2 (7p). LJ to top (see Photo C). Do not RW.

PHOTO C

Rnd 2: Ch 15. LJ to 4th p of prev rnd.

Ch 5.

Using SH 2, R 4-4-4-4. Then resume working with SH 1.

Ch 3, bp of 3 seed beads, Ch 2.

Using SH 2, R 4-4-4-4. Then resume working with SH 1.

Ch 2, bp of 3 seed beads, Ch 3.

Using SH 2, R 4-4-4-4. Then resume working with SH 1.

Ch 5. LJ to 4th p of prev rnd. Ch 15. LJ to top (see Photo D). Do not RW.

PHOTO D

Rnd 3: [Ch 2, bp] 8 times, 2. LJ between chains of prev rnd.

Ch 6. RW.

R 3+3 (j to first p of first R of prev rnd).

Ch 11. RW.

R 4+4 (j to 2nd p of first R of prev rnd). RW.

Ch 11. RW.

R 3+3 (j to 3rd p of first R of prev rnd). RW.

Ch 9. RW.

R 5+5 (j to 2nd p of 2nd R of prev rnd). RW.

Long beaded p of 4 seed beads, dagger bead and 4 seed beads. Ch 9. RW.

R 3+3 (j to first p of 3rd R of prev rnd). RW.

Ch 11. RW.

R 4+4 (j to 2nd p of 3rd R of prev rnd). RW.

Ch 11. RW.

R 3+3 (j to 3rd p of 3rd R of prev rnd). RW.

Ch 6. LJ between Chs of prev rnd.

[Ch 2, bp] 8 times, 2. LJ to top.

FINAL RING
Note: Work ends into this ring.

R 6, j to jump ring, 6.

FINISHING
Finish ends of ribbon with ribbon crimp ends. Add clasp with jump rings. ∎

Annie's ® *Tatted Jewelry* is published by Annie's, 306 East Parr Road, Berne, IN 46711. Printed in USA. Copyright © 2011, 2013 Annie's. All rights reserved. This publication may not be reproduced in part or in whole without written permission from the publisher.

RETAIL STORES: If you would like to carry this pattern book or any other Annie's publications, visit AnniesWSL.com.

Every effort has been made to ensure that the instructions in this pattern book are complete and accurate. We cannot, however, take responsibility for human error, typographical mistakes or variations in individual work. Please visit AnniesCustomerCare.com to check for pattern updates.

ISBN: 978-1-59635-420-3

2 3 4 5 6 7 8 9